T0017809

Eruption!

FIRST EDITION
Series Editor Deborah Lock; **Editor** Pomona Zaheer; **Art Editors** C. David Gillingwater, Dheeraj Arora;
Senior Art Editor Clare Shedden; **US Editors** Regina Kahney, Shannon Beatty; **Production Editor** Siu Chan;
Producer, Pre-Production Francesca Wardell; **Picture Researchers** Marie Osborn, Sumedha Chopra;
Jacket Designer Natalie Godwin; **DTP Designer** Anita Yadav; **Managing Editor** Soma Chowdhury;
Managing Art Editor Ahlawat Gunjan; **Indexer** Lynn Bresler; **Reading Consultant** Linda Gambrell, PhD

THIS EDITION
Editorial Management by Oriel Square
Produced for DK by WonderLab Group LLC
Jennifer Emmett, Erica Green, Kate Hale, *Founders*

Editors Grace Hill Smith, Libby Romero, Michaela Weglinski;
Photography Editors Kelley Miller, Annette Kiesow, Nicole di Mella; **Managing Editor** Rachel Houghton;
Designers Project Design Company; **Researcher** Michelle Harris; **Copy Editor** Lori Merritt;
Indexer Connie Binder; **Proofreader** Larry Shea; **Reading Specialist** Dr. Jennifer Albro;
Curriculum Specialist Elaine Larson

Published in the United States by DK Publishing
1745 Broadway, 20th Floor, New York, NY 10019

Copyright © 2023 Dorling Kindersley Limited
DK, a Division of Penguin Random House LLC
23 24 25 26 27 10 9 8 7 6 5 4 3 2 1
001–333441–Apr/2023

A catalog record for this book
is available from the Library of Congress.
HC ISBN: 978-0-7440-6742-2
PB ISBN: 978-0-7440-6743-9

DK books are available at special discounts when purchased
in bulk for sales promotions, premiums, fundraising, or
educational use. For details, contact: DK Publishing Special Markets,
1745 Broadway, 20th Floor, New York, NY 10019
SpecialSales@dk.com

Printed and bound in China

The publisher would like to thank the following for their kind permission to reproduce their images:
a=above; c=center; b=below; l=left; r=right; t=top; b/g=background

Alamy Stock Photo: Robertharding / Roberto Moiola 19tl, Science History Images 42, Westend61 GmbH / Fotofeeling 6-7;
Dorling Kindersley: Jamie Marshall 18bl; **Dreamstime.com:** Ddkg 23tr, Evanfariston 22, Tearswept 36crb;
Getty Images: Moment / Albert Damanik 20crb, Moment / Jose A. Bernat Bacete 21, Moment Open / by Mike Lyvers 19cr,
Jim Sugar 1; **Shutterstock.com:** Dirk M. de Boer 43cra, cktravels.com 23b, Anton_Ivanov 29, James Davis Photography 27,
Liudmila Legkaia 34-35, Rubi Rodriguez Martinez 18clb, Benny Marty 41b, Stephen Reich 4-5, Alfiya Safuanova 24tr, Lia Sanz 7crb

Cover image: *Front:* **Getty Images:** Jim Sugar; *Back:* **Dreamstime.com:** Ekaterina Mikhailova

All other images © Dorling Kindersley

For the curious
www.dk.com

Eruption!

Anita Ganeri

Contents

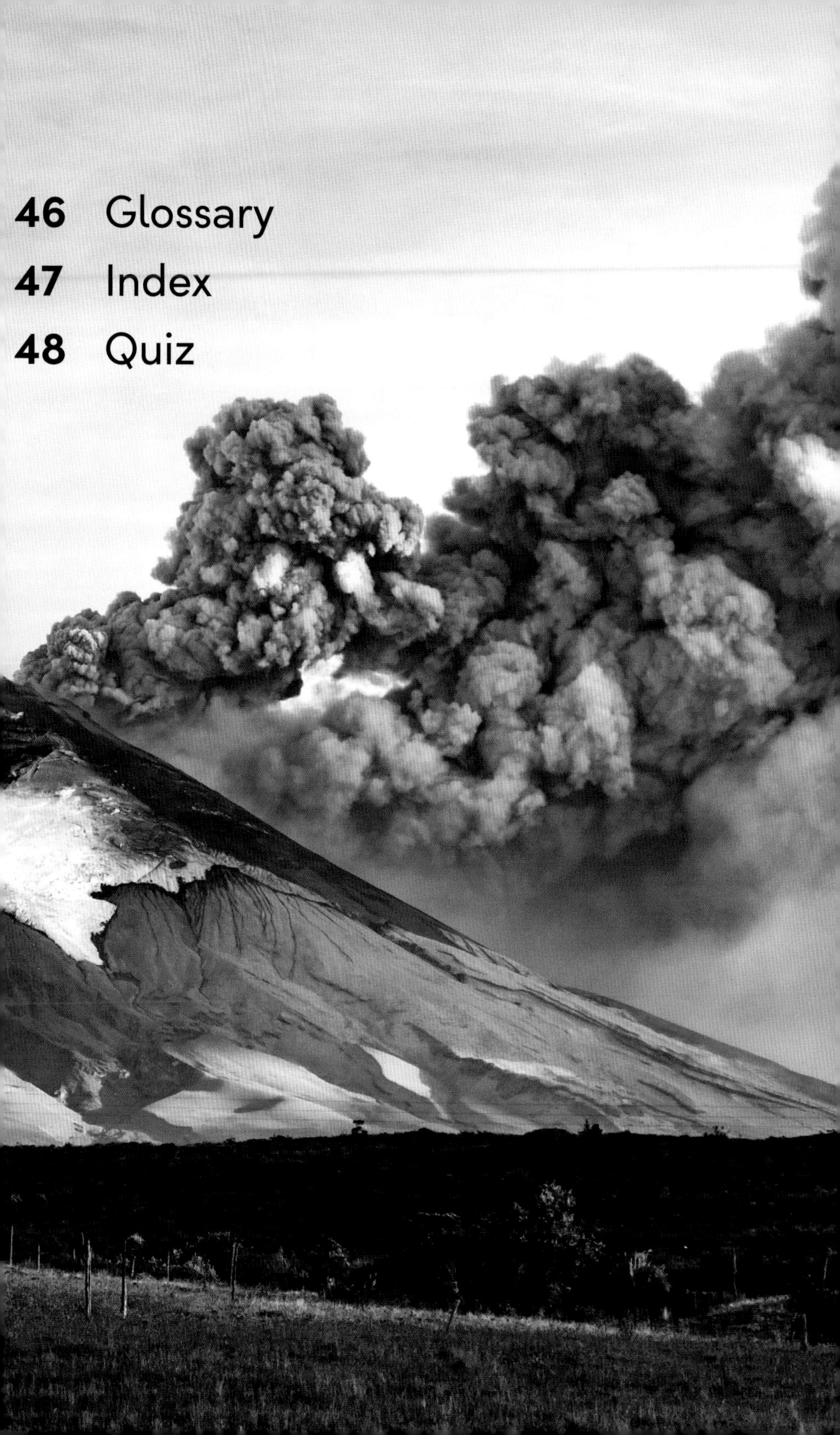

Be a Volcano Ranger

Go on real adventures!

- ☑ Learn about volcanoes.
- ☑ Help to take care of volcano national parks.
- ☑ Share your learning with others.

Things you can do:

- ☑ Watch an eruption from a safe distance.
- ☑ Collect interesting volcanic rocks.
- ☑ Hike to the rim of an extinct volcano.
- ☑ Walk through extinct lava tubes.

volcanic rocks

What looks like a mountain but spits out fire? What shoots clouds of smoke from a hole in its top? What sometimes explodes with a **BANG?**

A volcano, and it's starting to erupt!

What Is a Volcano?

The story of a volcano starts underground. If you jump up and down on the ground, it feels solid and hard.

But far inside Earth, it is so hot that the rocks melt. The rocks are runny, like melted butter.

Sometimes, the melted rock, or magma, bursts up through a hole or a crack in the ground. This is how a volcano begins.

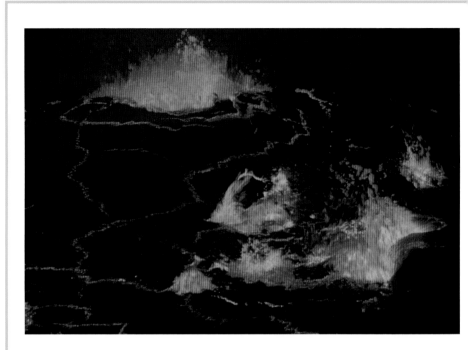

The melted rock that comes out of a volcano is called lava. At first, it is runny and red-hot. It cools down in the air and turns into hard, black rock.

Some volcanoes spurt out fiery fountains of lava. Other volcanoes pour out lava in great rivers of fire.

cooled lava

Once the lava starts flowing, nothing can stop it. It can bury whole villages and set trees and houses on fire.

Tectonic Plates

Earth's surface is made up of large slabs of moving rock called tectonic plates. These plates pull apart, slide past each other, and crash together. These movements can cause volcanoes to erupt and earthquakes to shake the ground.

Make a Volcano Model

To make an erupting cone-shaped volcano, you will need: a bottle, a tray, sand, baking soda, red food coloring, dishwashing liquid, and vinegar. You can decorate your volcano with plants, stones, and toy animals.

1. Place the bottle on the tray.

2. Build a mound of sand around the bottle. Keep the hole open.

3. Now place plants, stones, and toy animals around the volcano.

4. Mix together the baking soda, red food coloring, and dishwashing liquid in the bottle. Then, pour in vinegar. Watch your volcano erupt!

Types of Volcanoes

Volcanoes have different shapes and sizes. Some volcanoes erupt with a bang. Hot rocks and ash shoot high into the air. These volcanoes form cone-shaped mountains with steep sides.

Other volcanoes erupt quietly. The lava oozes gently out of the top and spreads out all around. These volcanoes are low and wide.

Cinder Cone Volcano

Cinder cone volcanoes spew lava that hardens and breaks into small pieces, or cinders. The falling cinders create a cone-shaped hill.

Composite Volcano

Composite volcanoes form as lava, ash, and cinders from previous eruptions build up over time. These large, steep volcanoes produce big explosions.

**Paricutin
Mexico
cinder cone volcano**

**Cotopaxi
Ecuador
composite volcano**

**Erta Ale
Ethiopia
shield volcano**

**Mount Lassen
California, USA
lava dome volcano**

Shield Volcano

The eruptions from a shield volcano are often slower than a composite's. Lava flows in all directions, creating wide slopes.

Lava Dome Volcano

Lava dome volcanoes form when lava is too thick to flow very far. The lava piles up over the volcano's opening, or vent.

Some volcanoes erupt violently. They blast out clouds of hot ash and dust. The ash is made of gas and tiny pieces of lava and rock.

Ash
It can be fine and powdery, or coarse like sand. Clouds of ash can travel thousands of miles away from a volcano. In 1815, when Mount Tambora in Indonesia erupted, ash spread around the world. It blocked the summer sun and caused parts of the planet to cool for several months.

The ash and dust shoot high into the air. Some of it lands near the volcano. It covers buildings and fields in thick, dark gray powder.

Some ash and dust is carried away by the wind. It can block out the sun and seem to turn day into night.

At the top of a volcano is a hollow called
a crater. In it is a hole called the vent. Lava,
ash, and dust come out of the vent. Some
craters are many miles wide.

When a volcano stops erupting, the crater
is left. Some old craters fill up with water
to form huge lakes. Sometimes, the crater
becomes a dry, grassy plain.

Crater Lake

Crater Lake in Oregon, USA, is the deepest lake in the United States. It formed when Mount Mazama, a volcano, erupted and then collapsed almost 8,000 years ago.

New Zealand's Emerald Lakes are crater lakes, too.

Stromboli

Lava shoots out of Stromboli, a volcano located off the coast of southern Italy, several times an hour. Stromboli is nicknamed the "lighthouse of the Mediterranean" because its fiery plumes can be seen from far away at night.

When a volcano shoots out lava and ash, we say that it is erupting. We call a volcano that is erupting "active."

Kilauea (KILL-uh-WAY-uh) in Hawaii is the most active volcano on Earth. It has erupted nonstop since 1983!

We call a volcano that is not erupting "dormant." That means it is sleeping, but it could erupt at any time.

Montserrat is a tiny island in the Caribbean Sea. It used to be a beautiful place to live. Then, in 1995, a volcano called Chance's Peak started to erupt.

volcanic ash

It had been dormant for more than 300 years. Many people had to leave their homes as ash fell everywhere. Some left the island and went to live in another country. It was too dangerous for them to stay.

Mount Vesuvius (vuh–SOO–vee–uss) is a volcano in Italy. In 79 CE, Mount Vesuvius erupted violently, blasting hot ash and gas into the air.

The ash buried the town of Pompeii (pom–PAY) and thousands of people died. Today, you can walk around the streets of Pompeii and see the Roman ruins.

A cast of a dog covered by the ash

The ruins of the Roman town of Pompeii

Record Holders

Many volcanoes are famous for their eruptions and size. Here are some of the record holders.

Dormant

Name: Mount Fuji
[Mount FOO-gee]

Location: Japan

Record: the world's most closely watched volcano

Dormant

Name: Mount Vesuvius
[Mount vuh-SOO-vee-us]

Location: Italy

Record: the world's most visited volcano

Name: Mauna Loa
[MAW-nuh LOW-uh]

Location: Hawaii, USA

Record: the biggest
volcano on Earth

Active

Name: Krakatoa
[CRACK-uh-TOE-uh]

Location: Indonesia

Record: produced the
loudest bang ever heard
when it erupted in 1883

Active

Name: Kilauea
[KILL-uh-WAY-uh]

Location: Hawaii, USA

Record: the most active
volcano on Earth

Extinct

Name: Olympus Mons
[uh-LIM-puhs mons]

Location: Mars

Record: the biggest
volcano in the
known universe

Volcanoes: The Bad and the Good

Volcanoes can be very dangerous and set off other disasters.

Earthquake
A volcano can sometimes set off an earthquake. Violent earthquakes can destroy cities and kill people.

Tsunami
A volcanic eruption can cause a giant water wave called a tsunami. The wave destroys everything in its way.

Weather Disruption
When a volcano erupts, gas and dust are thrown up. This can blot out the sunlight and cause strong winds and heavy rainfall.

pumice stone

However, they can also be useful.

Rocks
Some volcanic rocks, such as pumice, can be used to rub away hard skin. Basalt is used to make building blocks and sidewalks.

Farming
Eruptions clear away old, dead plants. Volcanic ash makes the soil rich for strong and healthy plant growth.

Hot Springs
In some volcanic regions, people use hot underground water to heat their homes and make electricity.

Buried Treasure

Diamonds can be found in a type of rock called kimberlite. This rock is formed from a rare kind of magma found way below Earth's surface. When some volcanoes erupt, they can carry these buried treasures to the top!

In some places, blocks of solid lava are used to build roads, bridges, and houses. Precious gold and diamonds are found in some volcanic rock.

Near a volcano, the underground rocks get very hot. The hot rocks heat up water, which turns to steam. Sometimes, a giant jet of boiling water and steam bursts up through the ground and into the air. The jet is called a geyser.

Old Faithful is a famous geyser in Yellowstone Park, Wyoming, USA. It got its name because it bursts up about 20 times a day.

Soaking It In

Volcanic hot springs, like geysers, come from heat inside Earth. This is called geothermal heat. In Iceland's Blue Lagoon, people can soak in water that is heated by lava fields. And in Japan, macaques, or snow monkeys, can relax in hot springs, too!

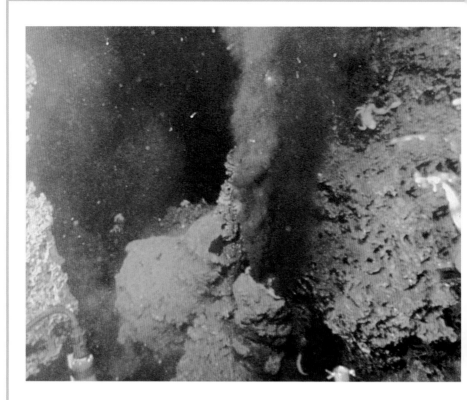

There are lots of volcanoes under the sea. You can't see most of them. But some underwater volcanoes are so tall that they poke up from the sea to make islands.

In 1963, a volcano erupted under the sea near Iceland. The sea started to smoke and steam. Not long after, the volcano had grown and a brand-new island had formed. The local people called it Surtsey, named after an Icelandic fire god.

Ring of Fire

Most of Earth's active volcanoes are located underwater along the edges of the Pacific Ocean. Called the Ring of Fire, this is actually a horseshoe-shaped area with more than 450 volcanoes.

Hawaii is a group of more than 100 islands in the Pacific Ocean. The islands are the tops of huge underwater volcanoes. Some of these volcanoes have two or more craters, but they erupt very gently.

In some places, lava flows into the sea and makes it hiss and steam. Some of the beaches have black sand, which is made from crushed-up lava.

Lava Tubes

Hawaii has a lot of lava tubes, underground passages created by flowing lava. These tubes can be active, meaning that lava still flows. An extinct lava tube does not have flow. The lava cooled and formed a cavelike tunnel.

Volcanologists are scientists who try to find out how volcanoes work. They want to know when volcanoes are going to erupt. Then, people living nearby can be moved to safety.

But volcanologists have not found all the answers yet. No one knows when a volcano will erupt—until it actually does!

At Work
Volcanologists measure a volcano's temperature changes and monitor the gases that come out of it. These scientists also use equipment that detects tremors, or movements, in Earth's crust.

Animal Detectors

In 2012, scientists noticed that just hours before Mount Etna in Italy erupted, goats became nervous and ran away. The scientists think that the animals may have been able to feel early rumbles from the ground and detect gases in the air.

Volcanic Myths

In myths, volcanic eruptions are caused by gods and goddesses.

Vulcan

In Roman myths, he is the god of fire and crafts. The word "volcano" comes from his name. Vulcan's Greek name is Hephaestus.

In myths, he hides away in his workshops, which are under volcanoes. There, he heats and shapes metals.

Pele

She is the Hawaiian goddess of volcanoes. The legends say that a volcano erupts when Pele gets angry.

Surtur

He is the Norse god of fire. The volcanic island of Surtsey is named after him.

Fuchi

She is the Japanese goddess of fire. Mount Fuji is named after her.

Glossary

Active
A volcano that erupts

Ash
Tiny pieces of volcanic rock

Crater
A dip at the opening of a volcano where gas, lava, and ash come out

Dormant
A volcano that has not erupted in a long time but will erupt again

Eruption
When lava and ash shoot out of a volcano

Extinct
A volcano that has stopped erupting and will not erupt again

Geyser
A sudden jet of boiling water and steam

Lava
Hot, melted rock that comes out of a volcano

Tsunami
A giant wave of water that can be caused by volcanic eruptions or earthquakes

Vent
A volcano's opening

Volcanologist
(VUL-can-AHL-uh-gist)
A scientist who studies volcanoes

Index

Quiz

Answer the questions to see what you have learned. Check your answers in the key below.

1. Where does a volcanic eruption start?

2. What is the melted rock that comes out of a volcano called?

3. What is the hollow at the top of a volcano called?

4. Which is the most active volcano on Earth?

5. What type of volcano forms when lava, ash, and cinders from previous eruptions build up over time?

6. What type of volcano forms when lava is too thick to flow very far?

7. True or False: There are lots of volcanoes under the sea.

8. What are scientists who study volcanoes called?

1. Underground 2. Lava 3. A crater 4. Kilauea 5. A composite volcano 6. A lava dome volcano 7. True 8. A volcanologist